JESUS MINISTRY

Calling an emerging generation to live out on earth the radical life & mission of Jesus!

Andrew P. Yeoman

All Scripture quotations, unless otherwise indicated, are taken from the HOLY BIBLE, NEW INTERNATIONAL VERSION® Copyright© 1973, 1978, 1984 by International Bible Society. Used by permission of Zondervan Publishing House. All rights reserved.

NAS - New American Standard. Scripture taken from the NEW AMERICAN STANDARD BIBLE, © 1960, 1962, 1963, 1968, 1971, 1973, 1975, 1977, by the Lockman Foundation. Used by permission.

Some Scriptures taken from King James Version

Darby Bible. Copyright© 1890, Darby Bible.

All references to Deity have been capitalised by the Author. All emphasis within Scripture quotations is the author's own.

Copyright © 2008 Andrew Yeoman

All rights reserved. No part of this publication may be reproduced, stored in a retrieval system, or transmitted in any form or by any means, electronic, mechanical, photocopying, recording, or otherwise, without the prior written permission of the publisher.

ISBN: 978-1-60383-127-7

Published by:
Holy Fire Publishing
717 Old Trolley Rd.
Atten: Suite 6, Publishing Unit # 116
Summerville, SC 29485

www.ChristianPublish.com

Cover Design: Dylan Tucker,
Colour Mafia. (www.colourmafia.co.uk)

Printed in the United States of America and the United Kingdom

Dedication.

To all youth, students and young adults who have responded to the call to be radical followers of Christ; to those of them who are called to serve and advance the Kingdom of God in either workplace ministry, fulltime ministry, at home or abroad. These messages are for you and in turn for you to give to others. With the words of God's soldier William Booth:

'The revolution now begin, Send the fire today!'

Acknowledgements & Thanks

Thanks to those who have prayed for me and been a Christ-like challenge and example to my spiritual life and thinking, among whom have been true fathers (and mothers) in the faith, especially Peter & Jenny Williams who have stood with us in prayer, encouragement, fatherly counsel and strength. Also acknowledgment to those who have been examples of radical Kingdom service and true friends and brothers to me: Bob Gladstone and Keith Collins. Also a note of acknowledgement to Dr. Michael Brown who through his passion for my generation and love for Christ helped form an environment of training in which I was truly set on track for the Lord. What God did in that environment *is* bearing, and *will* bear lasting fruit for years to come!

To all the young people of Europe Ablaze & Kingdom First Training Centre who have shared with us in the Gospel and have opened their lives to the things of the Holy Spirit. You are all, down to each and every person, precious. Every individual is special to me. Each called of God for such a time as this. Also thanks to the leadership and body of believers at SVBC for being a people who obey His voice. Thanks for praying, believing and being a strength.

My love and gratitude also to the gracious people of God in Poland. Thank-you for your reception and openness to God. May God touch the land in power.

Thanks also to the proof-readers: our fellow labourers and dear friends Ceirion and Katie Harris, and our good friend Barny Harper (Mr

English). Thanks also to Dylan Tucker for his expertise in design, and all the time and skill so generously given.

Thanks to all the family, including my parents, Peter and Lynne Yeoman, who not only brought me into the world but brought me up in the blessings and covering of 'a house of a Levite.' Thank-you for obeying the Lord and planting a little church in an aqua-green shed. Little did we know then what God had in mind - and yet your persistent spirit, determination and ability to 'get back up again' have been used by God, and have caused that little gathering to become an Antioch.

My deepest love and gratitude go to my precious wife Helen. You are my gift from God, my balance, my helper, my love and my best friend. These have been the best days of my life! Your strength in Him is remarkable, you have proved God time and time again, and you inspire my faith for breakthrough wherever we go. You are a 'winner'! I'm so glad we are in this together. God has been good to me. There is a new pasture ahead, let's enter with faith!

Most of all my worship and adoration go to God.

He has been a patient Father in dealing with me over the years and has been faithful to perform that which concerns me.

King Jesus - He is my all, my salvation, my righteousness and reason for living, the call to follow still breaks me.

Holy Spirit - thank you for your awesome presence, the way You have been with me always through the dark moments, in giving me the light of His Presence and Word. YOU are the Spirit of Wisdom and Revelation!

Contents.

Foreword by Bob Gladstone 15

Introduction 21

Chapter 1: A Revelation of Jesus (Part 1) 27

A call to the young church of the West - now blinded by secularism and gimmicks - to see with clarity the glorious Christ of their salvation.

Chapter 2: Divine Possession 43

Seeing that we are not just saved to get into heaven, but rather to become a part of something unique and bringing others into that end time goal - the Spirit filled people of God.

Chapter 3: Otherworldliness 59

The infiltration of the spirit of the age has clouded who we are meant to be in Christ - are we an eternal people bringing an otherworldly message and alternative lifestyle of the Kingdom?

Chapter 4: Jesus Ministry 83

In the proclamation of the Gospel both at home & in the nations, dying people in gross darkness do not need social justice alone, rather they need to have Jesus revealed and demonstrated through His body in the power of the Spirit, thus announcing the arrival of His Kingdom to them!

Chapter 5: A Revelation of Jesus (Part 2) 93

Peter had the revelation of Christ as Son of God, upon which the Church is built. Paul saw the Risen Lord and heard His commission to 'Go'. John saw the Christ, Lord of history past, present and future and strengthened the Church to endure in the epic battle for the Gospel of the Kingdom. All three were apostles; they prepared the saints to be apostolic. Will we choose to see a fresh glimpse of the Lord and be consumed with His desire for the apostolic Gospel to be proclaimed among the nations?

Chapter 6: The Dream 109

Can there be a true Spirit-born revival? Are we open to reformation in the Church? Can it be a move of revolutionary proportions? It's time to end the talk and begin to obey the commission!

Chapter 7: Jesus People 119

Like the Children of Israel wandering in the wilderness, many today receive from Him, hear Him, and see His miraculous ways, yet the meaning of the future move of God is to capture the real essence of becoming a 'Jesus People'!

Appendix 1. 147

Appendix 2. 151

Notes 153

Foreword.

With all my heart, I believe this is the year of new beginnings for the Church and the nations in the West. We are about to enter a spiritual Promised Land as we exit a kind of spiritual desert. A self-centred gospel, humanism-centred churches, celebrity-centred ministries, and even sin-centred living have too often characterized the previous generation's Christianity.

Forty years ago, a wicked cultural revolution swept America and Europe. Sadly, it largely swept Western Christianity as well, leaving behind a spiritually weak Church and a morally dilapidated society. But those forty years are over. God is calling a new generation of youth to a *Jesus*-centred Kingdom. They are about to experience the living God-Man, Jesus Christ, in a fresh, transforming way. Thus they will embody a different kind of revolution – a spiritual revolution, a *Jesus Revolution* – and will powerfully bear witness to Him among the nations. A mighty army is rising. A harvest is coming. Reformation is at hand.

Recently Lou Engle wrote, "there are moments in history when a door for massive change opens and great revolutions for good or evil spring up in the vacuum created by these openings. In these divine moments, key men and women and even entire generations risk everything to become the hinge of history, the pivotal point that determines which way the door will swing." We are now in one of those moments. The prophetic statement in my first paragraph demands a people worthy of the call and willing for the price. And it demands leaders who will lead with understanding of the times, purity of heart, burden for their generation, and courage for battle. I believe Andrew Yeoman is one of those emerging leaders.

This little book is a collection of penetrating messages that comprise a seven-fold apostolic appeal and prophetic call to a generation. It is a call to the youth of this generation for another great awakening across Europe and the world. It is a call…

1. To abandon "Christianised humanism," confess our utter helplessness, and seek

God as desperately as we really need Him.

2 To step into our identity as God's Spirit-possessed people.
3 To preach an otherworldly gospel under the anointing of the Spirit.
4 To incarnate Christ's own ministry of radical redemption for the world.
5 To see Jesus Christ as He really is, allowing that vision to transform us into apostolic people.
6 To feel God's own burdened heart – and dream – for this generation. And,
7 To enter courageously into the purpose of divine visitation: absolute union with Jesus and His followers for the sake of truly becoming the "Jesus People."

Will you hear this call? History truly depends on

it. You'll never be the same!

So gladly do I commend Andrew's book to you. He is a real soldier of the cross whom God is raising up amid this generation. It was my privilege to have him as one of my students for some months at the Brownsville Revival School of Ministry. More so, it has been my privilege to have him as a friend and co-labourer in the Kingdom for several years. I know first-hand that he is intimate with the Lord, pure of heart, deeply-burdened, filled with integrity, and consumed by God. He is a genuine servant of the Lord for this hour. His messages contained in this book hit some of the ultimate, necessary issues confronting today's Church. They're charged with a God-given burden and passion. And they're anointed with the Spirit of wisdom and revelation, coming out of a life of brokenness and intercession.

Read it carefully as I have. Let the messages sink in and change you. Let them encourage you and cut you where necessary. God wants you to be like His Son, Jesus. These messages are a tool He can use to serve that purpose in your life! Will you let Him? After all, the Church needs you. History has opened a door to you. There's a brand new Jesus People rising right now! Don't let this moment pass you by. He's calling. On with the Revolution!

Bob Gladstone
Director, FIRE School of Ministry
Concord, NC USA

Introduction.

This is not a long book. It has been put together with a sole purpose in mind - to spark something in the youth of today that will lead to a genuine move of God, of a 'reformational' kind. Contained in this short book are a collection of messages that have been spoken to either the student / young adult's group that meet each week at Swansea Valley Bible Church, or during similar events in other European nations. I am very aware of this book's shortcomings, especially as it's the first one I have ever written. Please forgive the rough edges and remember that it is not a book written as a progressive message, but rather a coalition of messages that have been abbreviated, adjusted and adapted for the sake of the young reader, with the aim of giving a brief taste of those things that burn in my heart for today's young people.

The precious groups to whom the message was given have known insignificance as far as the limelight of the world is concerned, yet have stood for the purity of the faith when all else was contrary. The key to this was not my leadership, neither was it our 'programme', because quite frankly we have never had one! Rather it was the powerful infusion of the Holy Spirit into our hearts as we collectively went after Him and the Master's voice to us in those moments. We don't profess to have the full revelation of God and His ways, neither do we think that these messages are God's final word to all. On the contrary, we feel that we have only scratched the surface of the deep things of God. Some of these messages have been a hard pill to swallow for us as we have realised the great cost involved in seeing the Kingdom come. As we have cried out to God in prayer and worship, He has been faithful to reveal Himself to us. At times Christ has stood among us through the Holy Spirit and His words have been Spirit and Life to us... and yet we have been all too aware that there is a price to pay. Even as we say this, we are far from having 'arrived' at that place we have desired to be. His command to BE His disciples and to GO where He sends is, even as I speak, still costly, still difficult and yet following Him is so much of a delight. We will reap, if we faint not!

I am also aware that this book may not be to

everyone's taste. Some may find it too deep or intense, whilst some may say it is too extreme for young people. All I can say in reply to this is, please seek the Lord with an open heart as you read. In my experience as a young person and a leader of them, I have found that we are actually crying out for a depth of encounter with the living Christ, and to know an intensity of relationship with Him, *beyond ourselves*. It is my experience that while young people may not understand all that God's word shares with them, when they come into these spiritual realities by experience, they will soon know the theology. Over centuries we have seen that revival has a way of revealing the deep of God to the young, and so it has been with the young I have had the privilege of serving. Our goal now is to see all consumed by the fire of His heart, come into revelation of His person and purposes, and serve Him with everything.

My prayer can only be that the Lord would make these few words Spirit and Life to you, and that as you read them, you too would know of the dealings of the Lord, His Word burning in your heart as it did in ours during those moments, and that you too would be set ablaze for Christ and His Kingdom!

Amen.

Chapter 1

A Revelation of Jesus (Part 1)

A generation that sees.

Cast your mind back. Can you recollect moments of great supernatural significance in the journey of your life? Moments that have transformed you and helped shape who you are today? I guarantee that if you've been following the Lord for some time now, there will have been such moments of Divine encounter or visitation. There is one man who recently wrote a book headed, 'A Lifetime of Prophetic Moments.'[i] I too, with him believe that a walk with the Lord Jesus is filled with those Divine moments of prophetic significance and fulfillment.

There are two of those kinds of moments in my life where the Lord specifically ignited my heart with the heading of this chapter. Both were related in that they were given in moments in which I was praying for the nation of Poland, the people of God there, and our work among them. On both occasions, it was as if the Lord reminded me that the only way believers truly become a New Testament people of movement is not through what men exhort them to do alone, but rather by God causing His people to see Him! This, of course, is not solely a Polish issue, but rather a spirit of dullness and blindness that hangs over both Western society and churches as a whole. It is one thing to acknowledge Him, believe in good theology and be a committed member of a Gospel preaching Church but there are times when we can lose the reality of the Spirit in our meetings, and in our private prayer lives and vision. Instead of having a freshness and clarity in our focus of the Lord, it can become a stale and comfortable affair. My prayer is that as you read this, something of that reality, reviving and clarity to your spiritual focus would take place in the eyes of your heart.

The Church in the West & the Laodicean problem.

Revelation 3: 18

'Buy ointment to smear on your eyes so that you may see.'

We read in Revelation 3 of the Church at Laodicea - a people of God who had become comfortable with their prosperous surroundings. Many quote this account of Laodicea and claim that they were lukewarm in their passion for Christ, and that He would rather they were cold (not for Him at all) or white-hot for Christ. Whilst being passion-less may have been one of the issues, it certainly wasn't what Christ was saying to the Church there. He was chastising their lack of effectiveness in being salt and light to the area. There were hot springs there that had definite benefits and there were cold springs there that had beneficial properties. But to be lukewarm was neither of the above, and it equaled ineffectiveness. To add to this the people of Laodicea could not see their pitiful state before God. The area was famous for its popular trade in violet garments. The city was also known for specialising in eye ointment and had become a major exporter of these things. Thus materially and financially, the area was flourishing. The people of God had probably become wrapped up in all of this materialism, and as a result had become a comfortable and lukewarm church; evangelical in tradition rather than evangelistic in activity, and *feeling possibly that they could embrace the ways of that city to win the people, rather than being God's alternative to the city!* They had forgotten that they were a people called from the darkness of the world to be the light of Christ, yet they considered themselves rich & abounding. *They did not realise that they were without spiritual sight and when you cannot see, you fail to realise the barrenness and ineffectiveness of your life for God!*

The Western attitude - 'We've got what it takes.'

There is a message being issued forth in this present day by those within the Western Church, that carries a familiar tone to the Laodicean way of thinking. Many of us have probably heard the rhetoric - *'God wants to release the greatness within you!'* Yet despite responding to the occasional emotionally-charged, concert-style meetings, the majority of people remain unchanged and undelivered, still held bound by the things of this life while attending Church. Like Laodicea, we have become confident in our capabilities rather than fully reliant in the power of the Cross and the Spirit. Church - we cannot see! When Christ came to touch lives with His Gospel, the overwhelming response of the people would be that of Godly sorrow leading to repentance; that great sense of sinfulness and emptiness without God; followed by that conviction that in Christ they could become new! Yet today there is little emphasis on the need to exchange the old for the new, for people are told they already have that which they need, and all that is needed is for God to 'bring out the greatness'. Young people we have been duped into a false message akin to the humanistic thinking of this present age. Rather than being or making disciples of a Divine Order, we have been guilty of being or making disciples according to our kind. Jesus said, ***'Follow Me, and I WILL MAKE YOU...'*** We need to die to self-serving, personal gratification and embrace Christ for who He is! Only in Him is there greatness! It is only the one dead to self, sin and the old nature who can be truly great in the

Kingdom. We need to see Him again!

Revelation 3

¹⁷ You say, 'I am rich; I have acquired wealth and do not need a thing.' But you do not realize that you are wretched, pitiful, poor, blind and naked.

Read those words again, *'But you do not realize.'* We need a revelation of Jesus again!

There is a story that comes from the Middle Ages, during the period when the Roman Catholic Church was the ruling movement at the peak of its dominance, power & material wealth. A godly monk, called Thomas Aquinas, was walking with a Roman Catholic cardinal who pointed around him to the grand surroundings while saying to him, "We no longer have to say 'silver and gold I do not have'". Aquinas quickly replied, "But neither can you say, 'In the name of Jesus Christ of Nazareth, rise up and walk.'"

Dare we fail to acknowledge our lack of sight for fear of feeling hopeless? If that's the case, then we truly no longer 'see Jesus', for just one glimpse was enough for Isaiah and Paul to cause them to cry out 'woe is me' and 'send me'.

Seeing our poverty in the light of His riches. (A word to young ministers of the Gospel and youth / student leaders.)

The European and Western Church needs to acknowledge her poverty and repent!

Be earnest, therefore, and repent. **(Rev 3: 19)**

O how it hurts to admit one's wrongdoing. I often remember my parents telling me on occasions that I had to apologise to those I had hurt or offended and put matters right. The wrestling in my heart in those moments was enormous as a child. I could barely get the words of apology out, so great was the crying and the enormity of facing up to people. In the same way it is a huge thing for 'Spirit-filled' believers, especially those of us that think we hold the correct doctrinal stance on the Spirit, (who can contain Him?) to admit their wrongdoing and lack. Yet the repentant heart is the only heart God responds to. According to **Psalm 51: 17:**

'A broken and a contrite heart, these O God, You will not despise…'

Seeing our need of what He has.

We must 'buy' from the Lord, not with what we have to offer, but with all we are.

Revelation 3

*[18] I advise you to **buy from me gold** refined by fire so that you may be rich, and **white garments** to put on so that your shameful nakedness may not be exposed, and **buy ointment** to smear on your eyes so that you may see.*

It takes a humble man or woman of God to acknowledge that they are naked and blind; it takes a man or woman of faith, true faith, to no longer rely on the talents they have, but to put all on the altar for the Lord. The fulfillment of true destiny is only realised when *we* reckognise it is only the Spirit of Christ *in us* that brings fruitfulness! I once knew a Godly brother who said, ' *The only thing that pleases God is what He does Himself.*' Oh, how we need God to empty us of our pride and self-sufficiency!

However, the Lord in His dealings does not leave His people with nothing when we come to Him. After seeing our lack in His presence, we become suddenly aware of His fullness. There is a Promise which is Faithful and True - a Promise in Christ of what is available to those that come back to Him:

- **The promise of Gold** refers to the pure Gospel - spiritual riches in Christ *for* the believer and *through* the believer to the needy. (i.e. His power / authority to extend the Kingdom.)
- **The promise of White Garments** refers to

the work of Christ and the Atonement. (i.e. our being identified with Him in His nature, death, resurrection and reign.)

- **The promise of Eye Ointment** symbolises the oil of the Spirit of God. The prophetic and revelatory Spirit that touches the true NT Church of Jesus, that they might become seers and recipients of the Spirit of Wisdom and Revelation.

I speak to those of you called to lead this generation, among whom I am one. Can we say that we have obtained that gold, those white garments and that eye ointment of which Christ speaks? Does the message we bear have that sense of Divine origin, and does it centre around the God-Man, Jesus Christ? Do the works we do demonstrate something obtained from God and

His Kingdom? Do we bring others into that same sense of seeing things eternal? That's our call as ministers of the Gospel. The Church has seen enough in the last 20-30 years of the various programmes instituted for young people - programmes that have 'wowed' the masses with loud and pulsating music, all brought by the latest cutting edge technology. Many of today's gatherings have been more about the latest teachings delivered in the slickest business-styled, motivational manner, than about a proclamation of the truth in substance & power. Ministers and leaders of this rising generation, listen to the words of Christ - 'be counseled to buy gold, white garments and eye ointment' - that we may see Him as He wants to be seen. Nothing else will do anymore. The Western Church is too strong, too worldly, too gimmicky and yet sadly wretched, blind and naked! The latest magazine styled conferences won't do it; the recent fad of motivational speaking rather than broken and anointed preaching won't do it. Come on young people, let us forsake these things and buy from HIM!

Some of you reading this may have believed in the Lord for many years or maybe you have just been attending Church yet not really knowing of that inner consuming fire and that vision of Jesus dominating your dreams and longings in this life. My counsel is to dare to humble yourself and seek the Lord. Dare we really listen to the voice of Christ to His Church and receive His counsel to buy from Him? Dare we surrender all the treasures of this life and self in order to buy those things that He makes available? Young person, are you really willing to be the only one who will pray and pursue the revelation of Christ? Are you willing to do this despite what others will say, even in a day when it is unfashionable to have prayer meetings or messages on purity or the deeper things of God in young people's events? Will you allow Christ to apply eye ointment to YOUR eyes? Is our generation in the Church willing to become as nothing, admit our lack and need of Him? I hope and pray so. It is a dangerous thing to ask to 'see'. It may mean we will become like Saul, (soon to be Paul) - one struck blind in order to be taught that all he needs for touching the nations is to see Jesus. O God let the cry of each heart be, *'Yes Lord - I want to see You.'*

Chapter 2

Divine Possession

A Generation of the Spirit.

There is an inner heart, there is an inner being, that can reach out, and you not only see the Lord Jesus but you feel the Lord Jesus... and you are one with Christ in an indissoluble union... you are part of Jesus Christ... you are one in Christ and with Him heirs of God.[1]

Hugh Black - Scotland.

Malachi 3 (NAB)

*[17] And they shall be mine, says the LORD of hosts, my own **special possession**, on the day I take action. And I will have compassion on them, as a man has compassion on his son who serves him.*

1 Peter 2 (1890 Darby Bible)

*⁹ But ye are a chosen race, a kingly priesthood, a holy nation, **a people for a possession**, that ye might set forth the excellencies of him who has called you out of darkness to his wonderful light…*

The term 'possessed' brings up all sorts of uncomfortable thoughts in our minds, especially when we read in the Scripture of those who were 'possessed' by evil spirits. In the Old Testament we read that the Spirit clothed Himself with Gideon. We do not hear enough today of the reason Christ died and shed His blood for us; that is the gift of His Spirit, poured out upon those who repent and believe. For this reason our God did this - that the Spirit may clothe Himself with a people! *This is why Christ came into this world… to get for Himself a people for*

His own possession!

All New Testament teaching has its basis ultimately in the mission and message of Jesus - the focus being on Jesus - the Messiah and Son of God, who through His death and resurrection brought about salvation for God's New Testament people. They would comprise of Jew and Gentile to form a last days community of disciples, living in the present time by the Spirit, as they awaited the final triumph of that salvation in the return of Christ. The first followers of Christ knew that the time of the Kingdom had been fulfilled and would be completed when Jesus returned. These men and women lived like all the issues of Jesus Christ dominated their very being. They were consumed with Him… possessed by Him and

His realities. They knew that they existed as God's people for that time - chosen, redeemed, possessed by God - as His end time people. There are a few things the early church lived out and are of vital importance to the present day disciple:

- Though our bodies still await that awesome time when Christ will return to perfect His work concerning us and make us like Him, our spirits have *already* been, and continue to be transformed (transfigured) toward perfection in Jesus. (Romans 8: 11). God is working His life into us *today*!

- God's people are to live in the sense that the glory of the future is already at work within them, both for the transformation of the person and for the preparing of the whole people of God. Heavenly eternity has been set in their hearts by the Spirit.

Ephesians 1 (NAS)

[13] In him you also, who have heard the word of truth, the gospel of your salvation, and have believed in him, were **sealed with the promised holy Spirit,** *[14] which is the first installment of our inheritance toward redemption as God's possession, to the praise of his glory.*

Listen to these words of revelation from Matthew Henry:

All who are designed for heaven hereafter are wrought or prepared for heaven while they are here; the stones of that spiritual building and temple above are squared and fashioned here below. And he that hath wrought us for this is God, because nothing less than a divine power can make a soul partaker of a divine nature; no hand less than the hand of God can work us for this thing. A great deal is to be done to prepare our souls for heaven, and that preparation of the heart is from the Lord.[2]

So then, what does this have to do with me, I hear you ask. Well, this generation has no sense of ownership and being. It has been said by one man that the present generation of young people in Europe are living in a vacuum, and that they are waiting for something or someone to come along and fill that vacuum. Young people want a cause with which they can align themselves (and give themselves to.) All we have to do is watch the present situation on the news to see that young men are giving themselves to false ideals and putting their hope and identity in a god who always demands yet never communes, who hides and never reveals himself.

When we, the emerging generation in the Church catch a glimpse of, and take a look *into* what Christ *has* done and *is* working in us, then we will begin to understand that *we are His,* and His for a purpose. That purpose is to call others to obedience to the Gospel and to being a part of His people, His own possession. It is to see those who are possessed by anything other than Him, come to know of the freedom that comes by the possession of His Kingdom as it enters their hearts. That's true identity, that's true fellowship and that's freedom! The European nations again need to witness a community of a unique kind, a community possessed by a King and His Kingdom - a demonstration that God is fashioning something here on earth for His eternal glory and the ages to come. Consider the impact - a Holy Sprit possessed generation, living out His life on the earth, for God's ultimate glory.

Jesus Himself was consumed and possessed!

Proverbs 8
²²The **LORD** *possessed me in the beginning of his way, before his works of old.* (KJV)

John 2

*17Then His disciples remembered that it was written, "Zeal for Your house **has eaten Me up."***

Consider this, that the Son of God was consumed and possessed with the Spirit of God and with the zeal of the Lord! At the age of twelve He was sitting with the scribes discussing the things of Old Testament scripture. Then at the beginning of His ministry He is charged by the Holy Spirit and led into a season of fasting. He said that His food was to do the will of His Father. Yes, Christ was the Son of God and yet He came as a man. Not only that but Jesus was a young man who was tempted in every point as we, and is now a high priest who knows our weaknesses. In all this He perfectly carried out the will of the Father with passion. Why? Because He was possessed by the Spirit of God constantly and completely.

In this generation of secularism within the Church where young men and women no longer have 'heroes in the faith' to imitate, then I say look unto Jesus Christ! - a young man who carried out His Father's will and is now exalted! He carried out all of this, for He was a man consumed, possessed and saturated by the Spirit of God and the will of His Father! Young people, imitate Him! Don't be consumed with passion for the things of this world which rob us of true identity and purpose but be possessed with Him! Let zeal for His house, His will and His Life consume you.

The surface level of merely acknowledging

Christ can become a deep consuming knowledge of Him.

There must be countless thousands of people who went through their younger years in a mere state of acknowledgment, yet regret the wasted years that God could have used in impacting their generation. I am convinced among today's present young generation that there are still those seemingly going through the motions of 'Christian life as they know it', without ever knowing the inner reality of God in their lives. I was one of those until God took a hold of me and led me and others through a time of deep disturbance from Him. During the Brownsville Revival, God took thousands of us young people and broke up the hard ground of our hearts and gave us hearts of flesh and a love for God beyond anything we had ever known. Even now, those of us touched by that revival should still evaluate our lives, and ask God if He still gloriously possesses us in a way that dominates our thinking and passion.

The very thing I am attempting to convey to you is best described in the following scriptures. In John 20 we read the powerful account of Mary's encounter with the risen Christ. I had always wondered about this story and meaning until the Lord spoke to me regarding it one day. Below are some notes I wrote of my own and collated from what I had read from others at that time:

i. **His command, "Touch Me not,"** is used in the present continuous tense, that is, it is to be understood as meaning "Do not hold Me" or "Do not cling to Me" (Jesus is not telling her not to touch Him per se, for we read the disciples had to touch Him later for proof of His resurrection.)

ii. **He diverts her** from the desire for previous relationship and conversation with Him at that moment of time. (Maybe she thinks Christ is risen in the similar state to Lazarus and will remain with them.)

iii. **'For I am not yet ascended,'** He says, **"unto the Father."** The former sporadic interaction is to be replaced by the new and continuous relationship in the heart that takes place in a deeper sense than before, but this cannot be until He is with the Father.

iv. **Christ is not there for restoring external things but for reconciling men to God.** He says, "Touch me not." Or - "Don't hold on to your previous limited knowledge of me. A new day has dawned!" (My words.) "For, though *I am not yet ascended, go to my brethren, and tell them, I am to ascend."* Jesus wants His disciples to look higher than his bodily presence, and look further than the present state of things and to now know HIM by His Spirit.[3]

In other words, at Christ's resurrection a deeper form of communion with Him could begin to be known. Now the possibility exists of a relationship beyond the mere external knowledge *about* Him, to a consuming union *with* Him. Awesome, glorious work of the Christ and Spirit! Young Christian you are called to know this!

Is this the kind of relationship you presently

have with the Lord? Leader, is this the kind of discipleship you seek to instill in the young people you lead? I speak from personal experience that the young people you disciple will only become what you *yourself* are. This is Christian discipleship of the unique kind, where the Spirit of Christ within forms and fashions His vessels of honour. This is the Jesus way - the way in which He Himself was possessed and consumed, so He now calls us to such a union. For a true move of God of revolutionary proportions, this is the only kind of discipleship - where Christ's nature is possessing our hearts, and we determine to follow! I finish with the words of C.T. Studd:

What a life the Spirit lives out in us when He possesses us. It is so simple too: just to remember 'I have been crucified with Christ,' I am dead. 'It is no longer I that live, but Christ that liveth in me.' My part is just to let Him live in me.[4]

Chapter 3

Otherworldliness

A generation of God's alternative to the world and the spirit of the age.

The evil age is to last until His return. It will forever be hostile to the Gospel and to God's people... we must strongly emphasise that God has not abandoned this age to the evil one. In fact, the Kingdom of God has entered into this evil age; satan has been defeated... We are caught up in this great struggle - the conflict of the ages.[1]

George E. Ladd

Revelation 19: 1 & 2

"Hallelujah! Salvation and glory and power belong to our God, for true and just are His judgments. He has

condemned the great prostitute who corrupted the earth by her adulteries. He has avenged on her the blood of His servants."

Ephesians 2: 1 - 6

*'As for you, you were dead in your transgressions and sins, in which you used to live when you followed the ways of the world and of the ruler of kingdom of the air, the spirit who is now at work in those who are disobedient. All of us lived among them at one time... but because of His great love for us, God who is rich in mercy, made us alive with Christ... And God raised us up with Christ and seated us **with Him in the heavenly realms in Christ Jesus.**'*

Babylon the great - the spirit of the age.

Many of us would have read or heard the

Genesis story of the tower of Babel at Sunday school or children's church and have for many years confined it to just 'one of those events' that happened in ancient times without seeing its significance. But the fact is, in the heart of mankind since the fall there has been the 'spirit that works in the sons of disobedience'. This is what was truly manifest at that moment in time.

That place where the infamous rebellion of man and God's judgment took place went on to be known as Babylon - *confusion.* It is then no great surprise that as we read Revelation 17, 18 & 19, the Apostle John sees a prophetic picture of a woman called 'Babylon' and it is her that is causing mankind to come under her influence and 'intoxicate' them with her sinfulness. Not only that, but to John it was revealed that she was being carried along by a beast. It's as if she thinks the beast is there for her purpose, but it in fact it's completely the opposite – he will one day show who he really is to her, and destroy her for his purposes. Babylon is the spirit of the age - the world that wars against everything a true people of God will be. The world / mankind think that they are in control of their destiny. The world believes that she can do without God and yet men will one day realise it was not them that controlled the spirit at work in them but rather it was the spirit at work in them that was controlling them! The beast is in control of Babylon and carries her unknowingly to her destruction. The Church stands as the City of God against this.

Do we see ourselves in the midst of such a

conflict? Do we truly understand the way the world hated Christ when He came to earth, and why the world should still hate us if we bear His image and message? It is because Christ was revealed at the right time to 'destroy the works of satan' in the lives of mankind. By His death and resurrection He has given man the opportunity to be freed from such slavery and to come into God's Kingdom. However the spirit of the age is violently opposed to that mission.

Those of you who are truly desiring to be that kind of person - one who bears Christ's mark and to glorify His name in the earth - YOU are in the midst of such a conflict! You are God's messenger representing His Kingdom. Your Spirit-filled presence on this earth is representing that unique life of another realm, as opposed to that which the world represents. For this reason they will hate you. Yet even in persecution, tribulation and even death, the Overcomer who has already lifted you to heavenly realms will one day vindicate His servants and triumph openly on this planet!

John 15: 18 - 19

"If the world hates you keep in mind that it hated Me first. If you belonged to the world, it would love you as it's own. As it is, you do not belong to the world, but I have chosen you out of the world. That is why the world hates you."

John 16: 33

"I have told you these things so that in Me you may have peace. In this world you will have trouble. But take heart! I have overcome the world."

The need of a true baptism of the Holy Spirit in this age.

If there is one thing my heart has grieved over in recent times is the apparent cheapening, watering down and emptiness of that experience which we claim is the 'Baptism in the Holy Spirit'. I don't intend to give the theology behind the various terms we should or should not use, but in the light of what we have seen regarding this conflict, we need to know something of the depth and power of this experience as it was known by the early Church. Above all else the early church knew the Christ they preached and the present and regular reality of 'The Presence'. New Testament scholar, Gordon Fee, rightly calls for the present day manifestation of this encounter as witnessed in the early church, even if we are still debating over technicalities.[2]

It is this firm belief and because of the definite encounter I had as a young child (and still have by His grace!), that I call my self unashamedly Pentecostal, not in terms of denominationalism or even in every part of its theology but in terms of recognising the reality and need for that which the early church and first generation Pentecostals experienced. Surely it was this experience and encounter that made them 'otherworldly.' We need to be immersed into God! My heart is often grieved when I see or hear of people who have had this glorious encounter cheapened. Whether it has been through the hyped-up emotions of the people or through the frenzied work-up of those 'ministering' to the recipients, much hype, danger and confusion has come into the experience of the recipient. Thus all too often, no true baptism has been experienced, no transformation has taken place, and God's Spirit has been grieved. We need honest words spoken in this hour of lack. We need a genuine experience if we are to 'walk this world in white.' It is no coincidence that when Jesus was speaking of the trouble and hatred of the world in John 14, 15 and 16, He also emphasised more than any other recorded time the work and ministry of the Holy Spirit. For this reason I want to raise the issue with young people living at this troublesome time in history.

If we will be hated on account of Jesus and experience trouble such as never has been known before, then above all things we must have the fullness of the Spirit in our lives. It must go beyond some of the shallow, and dare I say it, worked up, experiences of the past to something genuinely sent from above! Nothing else will hold us and make us to be all He desires us to be! I believe this is one of the reasons there is no 'otherworldliness' in the Western Church at present, because of the lack of genuine encounter with the Lord by the Spirit. I have witnessed in those I've had contact with, that they are filled and consumed according to the depth of hunger, thirst and seeking after this thing. During those moments I have also witnessed the following things when seeing God consume individuals and groups with His holy fire:

- A transformation from a mere passive

believing in God to a consuming love for Him.

- Something visible takes place and the glory of God is seen upon one's face.
- Most of the time initially, the person/s will speak in tongues as a sign with a supernatural anointing. (All Spirit-filled believers are empowered to speak with tongues.)
- Their worship and prayer life is transformed.
- A new passion for purity and Christ-likeness is evident.
- A heart for the Church, the Nations and for God's Kingdom is felt.
- A hunger for reality, and the truth of Spiritual power is sensed.
- Most of all, an unseen yet known, Divine reality is now transforming that person into

Christ likeness - which is 'otherworldliness'.

Without labouring this point, I just want to stir you to consider these things. Do you long for such a manifestation in your life and Church? Are you willing for the Holy Spirit to become the guiding Person in your life? Are you really longing for such an encounter?

If your answer is yes to these things, then you are a candidate for service in God's purposes. You are also a candidate for a very real assault on your life by the powers of the air that are so against the Lord and His own. Yet you will be one through whom God will delight to reveal eternal things to this present secular age.

The Glorious Gospel.

If our faith is secular it is because of the worldly-tinged Gospel now preached. If worldliness is present in 'Christian' young people today, it is because our message has ceased to be of another realm. One sure cause of spiritual decay in the land is the watering down of the Gospel of Jesus Christ. When our private spiritual life begins to wane, the cutting edge of our message is blunted and true effectiveness is lost.

Let's not be guilty of making such a mistake. This Gospel we preach and demonstrate is the Gospel of the Kingdom. That is, it is from above and ruled by above. Yet *we dare* to water it down, temper it or even (God forbid) become selective in what we deem its content should be! No. The Gospel of the Kingdom shall be preached in all Nations, then the end will come. It must be so, else we delay Christ's coming. The Gospel of the Kingdom stands alone in it's uniqueness!

Times change, people change, cultures change, styles change, language changes and even ways of doing things can change yet I believe there are some key ingredients to the Gospel that we should never lose. Too much has recently been lost in ministry for the sake of relevance and contemporary thinking. Here are some things that are for all seasons, times and peoples:

- The Person of Jesus Christ; God as flesh crucified; Risen from the dead, Ascended and Enthroned; Lord and King; The only

Way to Salvation; and the One returning to reign and judge.

- The complete depravity and sinfulness of mankind. (As opposed to 'how great we are'!)
- The Person of the Holy Spirit; the power of God to convict, convince, change, deliver, heal and fill. The only true ministry that makes the Gospel powerful.
- The Love of God and the Judgments of God.
- The message of repentance, forgiveness, new birth, adoption, eternal life and receiving the Spirit.
- The need of purity and holiness in God's people by the Spirit filled life. Complete separation from the world.
- Making disciples according to the pattern of Jesus, taking up our cross to follow Him

until death.
- Being salt and light to the world.

These are just some of the pillars of the faith! Sounds radical in a day when accepting Jesus and carrying on our merry way is preached? That's because it is. It is as radical today as it was when Jesus first began to preach, teach and do.

And yet, in case we think that we can just throw in the right phrases 'to make it happen', I have seen in my own life that all is in vain if I do not walk in true faith in the Lord and live in His life of the Spirit. Believing in doctrine will not save you. Believing in Jesus will. It is this 'thing' alone that makes the message of the Gospel so glorious, that God, *because of His Son Jesus*, now gives the repentant sinner, regardless of background, His own Holy Spirit and makes them His sons and heirs of the Kingdom! That is the miracle of the Gospel. Jesus IS the glory of the Gospel. It is this that must be preached in all nations of the earth, as our Lord commanded.

1 Corinthians 2: 6 -8

'We do, however, speak a message of wisdom among the mature, but not the wisdom of this age or of the rulers of this age, who are coming to nothing. No, we speak of God's wisdom that has been hidden and that God destined for our glory before time began. None of the rulers of this age understood it, for if they had, they would not have crucified the Lord of glory.'

Young saints, the message we have been

given is not of this world, even though it entered this world to redeem it. If it were of this age, the powers of darkness would have influenced it (they seemingly *are* in many circles) but because it came from the heart of God, the powers of the age could not grapple with it. It is this otherworldly message that has been given to us - pure and unadulterated. Ministers, what do you preach to the young people over whom you serve? Do you seek to appease their carnal appetite by 'putting on' that which they crave? Do you seek to make the challenge of the Gospel more palatable to their taste? Or is it a word brought from the King and does it carry His authority and power?

Young people I challenge you for the glory of God to live this otherworldly lifestyle according to the Word and preach this glorious Gospel by the power of the Spirit, and see what God will do through you even in this time of heightened sin and worldliness. Be that otherworldly ambassador for Jesus Christ!

The Glorious Gospel is that God has a Name!
One of my father's favourite sayings lately is, 'God has a name!' This is the ultimate glory of the Gospel, that God Himself has acted in human history and revealed Himself through His Son, JESUS CHRIST!

The angel told Joseph before the birth of the Christ, that His name would be Jesus, for He would deliver His people from their sins. We often quote this and other verses like it by using the word 'save' or 'saved' but when we use the original text we see how really awesome He is and how dire our need of Him is. The name given to the baby in Matthew is 'Jesus - deliverer!' Young people, we need His delivering power in our meetings. Deliverance from sin, self and this world's hold - does our message proclaim this kind of God?

And yet knowing this (as stated in denominational statements of faith,) our mainstream denominational youth departments are referring to the One who has chosen to reveal Himself by a Name above all names, to merely as 'God'. Even the demons believe there is a God, yet it must go further, deeper and become clearer in a shallow and unclear age. It was Paul Washer who recently made reference to Western Christianity being three miles wide and only an inch deep. God forgive us.

Youth leaders - if you preach God without His Name revealed, then the message is already diluted and becoming emptied of its power. His name is Jesus! Unashamedly, unmistakingly and definitely!

Whose side?
So then Babylon (the present evil age) is warring against the Kingdom of God and its people. It hates her and the Christ she loves and represents. It hates her glorious message and the very God who the message reveals as Jesus Christ. It despises those genuinely baptised in the Holy Spirit. Make no mistake, we are an eternal people, living out another Kingdom in an age and world that opposes everything

Christ is.

Is it clear as to whose side we actually represent, or is the line of divide indistinguishable in our church's activities? Are we a people of the age to come living in this world, or are we a people of the present age wanting to gain access into the age to come? God has set the mark of otherworldliness through His Son named Jesus and His radical, clear-cut message. *Whose side are you on?*

One final point.

To close this chapter, I wish to add only one thing that is given in answer to those that claim that the previous words will make the Church 'too heavenly minded for any earthly good'.

While those who have used this cliché in recent times may have meant to convey something of a truth, there is no doubt this statement has produced a conflicting strain within the body of Christ. I have witnessed on the one hand a great move of God that caused many thousands of youngsters to be taken up with everything eternal and with Jesus Christ. I have seen and heard of the dramatic impact they have made for the Lord in their generation. I have also witnessed the ebbing of this thinking as a time comes when satan throws out the accusation that they are too consumed with God and heavenly minded to be of any earthly use. When reading the book of Acts, if there is one thing that stands out above everything else, it is the 'otherworldliness' of that people called 'The Way'. They were providing the Gospel and reality of God as the relevant answer to the world's problem of sin and darkness. We must follow their example - our job is not to provide the world's answer to the world's question. The people of the faith *then* provided the real alternative in Christ. The people of faith *today*, must do likewise.

Today, men have become less concerned with the Glory of God among the Nations and more concerned about being 'sensitive' to the seeker. I end this chapter with the words of the late brother in Christ, Art Katz:

Paul not only found this eternal dimension, he also dwelt in it, and yet that did not condemn him to irrelevancy. On the contrary, it made him all the more relevant, and so it will make us also.[3]

Chapter 4

Jesus Ministry

A generation who are an extension of who He is.

It is not the Church's business in this world to simply make the present condition more bearable; the task of the Church is to release here on earth the redemptive work of God in Christ.[1]

LaSor

We are all familiar with John 14: 6. Jesus - the only way, the truth and the life. Yet few of us are probably aware of the equally significant words that follow from the Lord.

John 14: 9 & 10

'Anyone who has seen Me has seen the Father...it is

the Father living in Me, who is doing the work.'

These words we can all accept, as they form a part of the central doctrine of the Faith - that Jesus is the only begotten Son of the Father - there is none other. But Jesus is saying more than just making a statement of truth. He is stating something of the power of what and who He is demonstrating, namely the Kingdom of God, and that God the Father is conveying Himself and His work through His Son. What's more, Jesus goes on to make a further point:

John 14: 12

'I tell you the truth, anyone who has faith in Me, will do what I have been doing.'

When speaking of the giving of the Holy Spirit,

Jesus explains further:

John 14: 20

'On that day you will realise that I am in My Father, and you are in Me, and I am in you.'

Do you see the point Jesus is making? Whilst we are not God the Son, as He is, we are sons of God through our Lord Jesus. Because the Holy Spirit is given, in the same way that Christ ministered the Father, we by the Spirit can minister Jesus through 'greater works'! This does not mean that we are God, nor does it mean we do this perfectly as our Lord did, but it does mean that because of the Lord's great work on the Cross and the giving of the Spirit, there is a way for us - His people and body - to minister Jesus to the world! Just as the Lord Jesus ministered God the Father, we by the Spirit can bring Jesus ministry to the people. Christ's physical remaining was precious and needed, but the ascension was vital, so that He could continue to act in a greater, wider way through people. It is the very life of Christ Himself that flows by His Spirit through pure and yielded people. That then becomes a glorious outflow of the life of God to those we minister to. Do we manifest Jesus to a needy world or do we manifest fleshly ideas of what that should look like? Ministry above all else is incarnational.

There have been many over-uses of the word 'Manifestation' in recent times. In many respects the word has become cheapened. Surely Noah Webster touched something of its true meaning when he described its meaning as,

The act of disclosing what is secret, unseen or obscure; discovery to the eye, or the exhibition of anything by clear evidence; as in the manifestation of God's power in creation, or His benevolence in redemption.[2]

Are we such a generation? Are we, as LaSor so brilliantly said, *'releasing here on the earth the redemptive work of Christ'*? Are we a genuine manifestation of Jesus Christ in the way Noah Webster described it? More searching than that, are we manifesting the Person of Jesus Christ as a very incarnation of who He is? If not, then how can we claim to be His body and Him the Head? God wants us to be living out a ministry that is as Christ Himself to a dark and dying world. That is what genuine ministry is - His very life issuing from His Person through those who are truly 'in Him' and a part of Him. This is where mission becomes powerful, when a people in darkness see the 'great light' dawning in their region because an obedient vessel has brought the message, life and reality of his or her Lord to them, and all because they lived in such a way that they knew He was in them and they in Him. This is an awesome communion and union with God. Do we really know of this reality young people? Do you long for this kind of union and expression?

There is an ancient Jewish saying found in the Law which states:

'the one sent is as the man who commissioned him,'[3]

This is indeed a great challenge. It will mean the complete stripping down of all that the flesh wants to be in prominence, impatience and dominance. It will also mean the complete weakening of ourselves for His grace to flow. I've had to learn this lately. My wife and I recently have gone through the most difficult stage of our life. She was suddenly struck down by a strange tropical infection in 2004, and what ensued the following four years was a complete emptying of our powers, our ideas and a growing awareness of the grace of God - expressed through His Kingdom power. There were moments of incredible darkness, but the Lord would always come by His Spirit and remind us of His union with us and us with Him. If it were not for this truth experienced, through reality, we would not have learned the priceless value of knowing this union worked out in life and serving the Lord. People, God wants to take us from being those who 'believe about' this kind of possession, to the unique kind of person who encounters and knows the very life of their God, living, dwelling and expressing Himself to and through them. This is why God allows suffering - to test us in the proving of this unbreakable union. Peter the apostle expresses something of this in his first letter.

1 Peter 1: 6 - 7

... you may have had to suffer grief in all kinds of trials. These have come so that your faith - of greater worth than gold, which perishes even though refined by the fire - may be proved genuine and may result in praise, glory and honour when Jesus Christ is

revealed.

The apostle Paul in 2 Corinthians 12, knew of weakness and he was thankful for it. He knew in that moment of complete nothingness that Jesus would be all the more expressed through him. That's awesome. That's apostleship in its truest sense - Jesus Christ, and only Jesus Christ being revealed through a vessel who is sent as His representative to a people to lay the foundations of Jesus Christ. In Galatians 1: 15 - 16, Paul said that it was God's pleasure to reveal Jesus in him. It still pleases God to reveal His Son through yielded vessels. Will you allow God to make you such a minister?

Church, above all else let us rediscover true ministry again - that is Jesus ministry!

Chapter 5
A Revelation of Jesus (Part 2)

A Generation of Apostolic seeing.

The issue of seeing is crucial... Everything presently conspires against it. The World wants to fill our eyes with all of its voluptuous images... It takes an apostolic determination to break that, to close out the things that are visible, and to focus on the things that are invisible and eternal.[1]

'To make that the basis for all our seeing is at the heart of the apostolic! Do we see this world as under judgment?'[2]

Art Katz, Apostolic Foundations.

What was it that caused the people of the Way

in the book of Acts to live the life of the Way in the way they did? What was the foundation of Peter's life that was so crucial to the Church's birth and foundation? What was it that caused Paul to be compelled to go to the nations with the message of the Gospel and the Spirit's presence? What was it that caused John to bring awesome prophetic insight into the dealings of God with mankind and bring assurance to the Church of her final triumph? It was the reality of a revelation they had of Jesus.

They were men who had seen the Master! Not merely a theology, or a tired cliché, but His very burning reality, manifested to them and dwelling in them. The reality of the Spirit was more real to them than the darkness around them and the world they lived in. They were truly a people of New Covenant perception. Is that how we see?

The one thing that will transform any group of indifferent or lukewarm people is to see Jesus - to have the 'eyes of the heart opened' and have revelation at the knowledge of Him (Eph 1: 17 & 18). It is this reality that causes the cold to become hot for Christ. When you see Him, the hard heart melts, 'like mountains as wax at the presence of the Lord.' The indifferent believer becomes a radical lover and follower of Christ and in their prayer and worship they go from half-hearted murmurings to passionate cries, and like John, fall as though dead at that revelation. When the Kingdom comes, the things of this world grow dim.

John - the apostle of seeing and knowing. *(The essence of a prophetic heart.)*

Let us consider John for a moment. If ever a portion of Scripture is alive with reality and life it is the opening words of John's first letter.

'That which was from the beginning which we have heard, which we have seen with our eyes, which we have looked at and our hands have touched - this we proclaim to you concerning the Word of Life. The Life appeared; we have seen it and testify to it, and we proclaim to you the eternal life, which was with the Father and has appeared to us.'

There is a sense in these words that John is not just describing the human side of Jesus (and of course that was a reality to him) but rather John is conveying that in a human shell dwelt the glory of God! Jesus - the radiance of the Father and the embodiment of eternal life! John had truly seen Jesus, not just the man but God Himself. The remarkable thing is that these were John's descriptive words of an experience of Christ *before* that which came to Him on the Isle of Patmos for the writing of Revelation. It is this that sets His vision and heart aright for what God is about to reveal and speak to Him later on in his life. In other words, you cannot see great visions of the things to come, unless you first *see* and are *touched* by the One who is Lord over that which has been in history, that which is presently, and that which is to come in the future. Again, in Revelation, the emphasis is the same:

17When I saw Him, I fell at His feet as though dead. Then He placed His right hand on me and said:

"Do not be afraid. I am the First and the Last. **(Revelation 1: 17)**

Prophecy is bound up in Jesus!

We may hear much today regarding the latest vision given to this one or that one, or the latest revelation or new thing God is speaking. In the midst of such things I want to affirm regarding seeing Christ - this is *the revelation* of the highest order, where one comes to such a glimpse of the Lord and knowledge of Him - the glorious risen Son, so that it sets them up, so to speak, for the rest of their lives. (In effect, it ruins them thus bringing true humility, desire and purity toward God.) Seeing Him in such a way as John did will cause true prophecy to be manifest in a life - for the testimony of Jesus is the spirit of prophecy. Today's shallow and often confusing prophecies are as they are because Christ is no longer the substance of our walk with God and thus He is very little to do with the prophetic word we so often hear about in services. It was Gordon Fee who said that, *'any kind of Spirit-talk that doesn't make the cross the heart of what we're doing, doesn't understand the faith at all.'*[3]

Young people - there is a place of seeing Christ and knowing Christ that you can come to despite your young age. Samuel, Jeremiah, Josiah, the Apostles are all young examples. Let our prayer be in this generation, *'O God I want to see You!'*

Paul - the apostle of seeing and going. *(The essence of a missionary heart.)*

'I was not disobedient to the heavenly vision', Paul declared to King Agrippa. Paul, formerly Saul, was a remarkable man on a remarkable mission. His *seeing* the glorified Jesus caused Him to see the *heart* of the glorified Jesus, that being the nations. When we examine Paul's life and those apostolic men of Church history, I am convinced that they were truly sent ones because they had seen 'the Sender'. It has been noted by one man that Paul did not refer to the prophecy received at Antioch in his commission to mission. As important as that moment was, it is noteworthy that it is never mentioned again by Paul, but the vision of the Lord on the road to Damascus is mentioned again and again! For Paul, his call was from Christ, through Christ and to Christ -

all in Him. Paul himself stated, not an apostle by the will of man but by the will of God. (Galatians 1: 1 & Colossians 1: 1)

It is no coincidence that the criteria for the first apostles was that *they had seen the Risen Lord*, for they were to be preachers and a witness of Christ risen from the dead. Let me ask this. If we believe in present day apostolic ministry (which I do), and that God has given such gifts to the Church, then why have men lowered the criteria of such a high calling? Today we have given such a sacred title to those that hold positions of administrative authority rather than those who function in His power. We have given credence to some kind of 'spiritual' entrepreneurs / managers, whilst forgetting that true apostles are a sent expression of Jesus

Christ, the one they have seen, handled, looked upon and the One who has undone them in every way. Today we look for the charismatic figure who has all the ability to hold such an office and yet Paul says of himself such words:

'I consider everything a loss compared to the surpassing greatness of knowing Christ Jesus my Lord, for whose sake I have lost all things. I count them as rubbish that I may gain Christ,' **(Phil. 3: 8)**

Paul's life was as good as dead after seeing Jesus. He was already in eternity. His one aim was to bring all peoples into that revelation. He wanted others to become what he himself had become. *'Imitate me...'* This is the heart of apostolic revelation - that which is seen - namely Jesus in His fullness - is declared, preached and passed on to all who believe and are obedient to the faith, even among the nations. Apostleship is a function of impartation, rather than just an office of position.

Paul's heart after seeing Jesus was for the peoples of the earth to come into the same 'dynamic' he had come into. For him, it was a matter of imparting a spiritual DNA into a newly formed people, in order that they imitate Paul, who in turn is like Jesus. It is this foundational ministry, which establishes strong communities of faith rooted in Christ. I believe this is the heart of apostolic mission & ministry.

For us, the life of Paul not only represents God showing Himself through a man in impossible situations on the mission field, but also Paul (then as Saul) being *himself* an impossible situation in the eyes of men, changed by the revelation of Jesus. When about to bring further warfare against the Church, he was undone by the Revelation. Do we fully grasp what God can do when a man or woman truly sees Jesus and believes His voice of commission to go, even if the situation is dark?

I have personally seen hard situations, sometimes impossible situations change for the better when God reveals Himself. My mind recalls a time when faced with fifty young people at a Polish youth camp. We had been asked to take a team to go and minister the Word for one week at a remote location in N.E Poland. Upon our first moments there we discovered that we were going to have to cry out to God for a breakthrough to come into this group of people or else all would fail. Some were cold and unsaved, some lived with a foot in the world while pretending to be spiritual. At best some loved God yet were so bound by those around. I remember the feelings among the team from Wales, some wanted to leave seeing the impossible task ahead. Being stuck in a remote place though made such an option impossible. We had to stay and prove God. We met the next morning and got on our knees, repented of our attitudes and cried out to the Lord. He heard our cry. The full force didn't come all at once but as we prayed day by day and cried out, a greater sense of God's power and Kingdom filled that camp until every person was consumed by it. Whatever we longed for God to do, He did, and more. Many were saved and still are serving the Lord today, many were filled with the Holy Spirit, some set free, some healed and ALL revived. Many of those young people continue to serve the Lord in a fresh and dynamic way till this day, all because the Spirit revealed Jesus and they were never the same!

In essence, this is apostolic activity. Men and women having a revelation of Christ; obeying His voice; being sent into the darkest of situations; causing others to see that same life-changing vision of Christ. Not everyone is an apostle in the biblical sense, but God's people are ultimately called to be apostolic. Young people, allow your heart to be captured by the revelation of Jesus. Allow God to make you one through whom revelation can be proclaimed.

Let our prayer be: 'Lord, let today's youth have a prophetic heart, an apostolic vision, and make known the revelation of Jesus Christ among all nations!'

Chapter 6

The Dream.

Can there be Revival, Reformation and Revolution?

'Jesus Lover of my soul, all consuming fire is in Your gaze... No one else in history is like You... You alone are God and I surrender to Your ways.' [1]

Paul Oakley

A religion, even popular Christianity, could enjoy a boom altogether divorced from the transforming power of the Holy Spirit and so leave the church of the next generation worse off than it would have been if the boom had never occurred. I believe that the imperative need of the day is not simply revival, but a radical reformation that will go to the root of our moral and spiritual maladies and deal with the causes rather than with consequences, with the disease rather than with symptoms.[ii]

A.W. Tozer

There has been much talk of revival in recent times. Much of the discussion has produced a healthy appetite for such a move, whilst some has created in Christians an unhealthy appetite for experiences and rhetoric that causes ears not to hear what the Spirit is truly saying. There is an element of this fervour that I believe the enemy has used, so that at times people have gathered together for the purpose of having such an experience rather than an encounter with the Master. As a result people talk little of hunger, passion, humility, prayer and purity; and, yes, even a complete surrender to God that denies the flesh, the world, sin and self. Instead you hear talk of instant signs that have resulted in a shallow, costless and blunt Christianity! One Welsh Revivalist notably said that in revival, Christ and Him crucified must be the centre of all fervour and spiritual activity. It is this that the Spirit bears witness to!

The dream.

In the Spring of 2004, I was in a season of desiring the Lord to speak specifically regarding a particular work that I was involved in. One Thursday, I remember trying to pray and read the Word, but found my heart hard to the Holy Spirit. That night I remember laying on my bed, about to fall to sleep, when I uttered these words, *'Lord, would you please speak to me tomorrow in regard to what you want to do in my life and generation?'*

In that state of an apparent feeling of nothingness in my heart, little did I know that these words had ascended quickly to the throne. That night I had a dream. I was visiting a particular nation with some of the missionary team I serve with, and we visited two of its major cities. Upon visiting the second city, we were held up because of the rush hour traffic. Eventually, we walked into this rather large University Hall, and waiting at the doorway was a man looking at his watch in an animated fashion. He began to reprimand us for being late, upon which I apologised and explained the reasons for the delay. He then became insistent that we needed to pray, and proceeded to guide us to a backroom. After the prayer time, we entered the main hall again and saw that it was filled with about 200 young students. I sat down and the Holy Spirit said to me, 'You are to speak about making a difference and being significant in the world.' At that point and to my amazement they began to sing a song about being a 'significance in the world' and about 'a revolution of the Kingdom'. I always remember the otherworldliness of that song, almost as if it were not written by men. As the song finished I looked to see who their leader was. I saw a man whose face I instantly knew. He was my teacher and president at a School of Ministry I attended - a man I greatly admired for having such a burden for my generation. He turned to look at me and after saying a few words to one another, we were strangely brought together to the point where we embraced and our arms were locked into one another's. Then it was as if the fountain of the Lord broke both in my spirit and his, and we began to groan, weep and cry out for the young people in the hall to know of a revolution in God. At this point a heaviness of God's manifest presence came down and all the students began to cry out intensely.

Immediately I awoke confused and wondered how this heavy, unearthly and holy 'feeling' I felt in the dream was still upon me in reality. I was dazed for a few hours that morning, knowing that somehow God had met with me, yet completely forgetting the prayer I had prayed the night previous. God had spoken. My life would never be the same again. For the following day I cried and cried as I told certain people close to me of the dream. God had met me in an unprecedented way and I was undone.

Christ the reformer.

A week after my dream I began to share with those I disciple and work with in missions. As we talked, that same nearness of the Lord came into the room and the Holy Spirit began to speak to people and melt hearts. We prayed and cried out, 'O God please bring change...let this generation do something of significance for You...'

For weeks after, we saw the life of our Lord in Scripture in a fresh way. We saw in a fresh way how He was and is our model for living a different life in this generation. Now He called for new wine skins to facilitate the new thing He wanted to do. We saw Jesus in a living and very powerful way bringing a revolution to people's thinking, an awareness of the Kingdom of God.

His ministry was with righteousness and power, yet ours had been weak, worldly and self-centred. He reformed us.

The revolution.

At present we are still knowing His reforming in our lives, and probably always will if we remain in Him. However, I am watching and praying closely because the signs of true change are beginning to emerge, as the early dawn skies light up just before the sun comes in view. You and I may never hear of any of these emerging young people who are beginning to respond to His call, but heaven knows them, and so too do the powers of darkness. Christ will triumph through them, even in tribulation, because He will build His Church. And though many of them may die in the flesh during service or may be criticised for their narrow way of living for Christ, they have His resurrection victory in their hearts. The Gospel will achieve its purpose in getting a people for the Lord and in crushing the serpent's head.

So where does this leave us? At the present point of writing, as I look to complete this book, I am looking at the years 2007 & 2008 with excitement and expectancy. The dealings of the Lord have been ruthless at times, and yet full of mercy. The year 2006 again we saw God begin to distribute gifts of His Spirit to the young people, and we clearly heard the voice from heaven commanding and commissioning us to do that which glorifies His name. Now it is time to obey and to do it. The nations need the light! I'm going. Will you respond to the call? Arise -

young army of the Lord!

'Why do the nations rage and the people plot a vain thing... against the Lord and against His anointed... I will give You the nations as an inheritance...'

Psalm 2

Chapter 7

Jesus People.

Will we wander and die during visitation or go into Jesus-centred identity during visitation?

"Do you still not understand?"

Jesus Christ (After feeding the thousands.)

I am convinced that to understand the true meaning of the Gospel disclosed by the New Testament writers, we have to get a grasp and revelation of the account of Israel's Exodus. Even more so, I believe the Exodus will have special spiritual significance in the life of the Church in these early years of this new millennium. Perhaps the Exodus is the key moment in all of Israel's history. It is central to their existence and understanding of the one true God and their role as His chosen people. I am a deep believer that it was with the Exodus in mind, the Gospel writers understood the emergence of Christ and His powerful victory on earth. In fact on the mount where He was transfigured and the disciples saw His glory, it is recorded that He spoke with Moses and Elijah regarding His 'departure' or *'exodus'*.

I believe that there are vital revelations deeply ingrained in the Exodus for the New Testament people of God. And to add to that, they will bear special significance and power in the imminent move of God that is about to break into the Western nations. At the time of writing there is a fresh excitement of imminent revival. It is as though Christ in His great compassion is about to feed the thousands, and cause a genuine move of the miraculous from the provision of His Kingdom. There are many signs beginning to take place among the hungry of heart. However, this move is about more than feeding the masses, good though that is. I believe God is speaking in the midst of this stirring, however only some may choose to listen to His voice. What is in my heart is in connection to the following question from Jesus.

"Do you still not understand?" **(Mark 8: 21)**

This is a monumental question from the Lord, after His disciples had just witnessed the feeding of the four thousand. Previously, they had seen the feeding of the five thousand, and so we must understand that their faith for this kind of miracle was not what was being questioned. Rather, Jesus was questioning their lack of insight into the signs and their deeper meaning. To get further insight into these events we have to look at John 6, where John the beloved disciple gives his own account of the feeding of the five thousand. He is the only Gospel writer who provides us with an explanation by Jesus of these unique feeding miracles. The two feeding miracles are closely connected. The message and meaning are the same, and yet each one is specific to those who witness them and are fed.

John recalls that after the first of the two miracles, Jesus is followed by the people. Jesus sees their hearts and knows that they are following because of what has just happened, not for who He is. Their cry is *"give us a sign and we will believe...*" In other words, they partake of His miraculous provision for their earthly needs, but will not see the miracles as manifestations of a spiritual truth. Jesus is the true 'Bread of life', which He embodies. He gives them eternal life through union with Himself. Jesus thus warns them for their lack of understanding in John 6: 49 & 50, and likens them to the early children of Israel who ate the miraculous manna from heaven in the wilderness AND STILL DIED! However, Jesus states that *He* is the true Bread of heaven, of whom men may eat and *never die*. But this is not the only thing Jesus is conveying here. He goes on to make further startling and even offensive statements to those around.

"Whoever eats my flesh and drinks my blood remains

in me, and I in him." **John 6: 56**

Jesus is here giving the *'deeper meaning'* of the feeding miracles. He is actually calling those that are pursuing His benefits, to go deeper and to partake of Him. *To eat the miracle bread is one thing; to eat of Him is the real deal!* In other words - it's a very awesome and deeply spiritual issue. It is not enough that we enjoy His awesome signs and visitation (although we are to rejoice when they happen!) but it is more an issue of experiencing the heart of visitation, through identifying with Him and becoming part of Him spiritually. To find that deeper meaning and experience in Christ is what it truly is to become His body - the one loaf.

The 'deeper meaning'.

Every move of the Spirit has one issue at the very heart of it. Despite their unique characteristics in each generation, whether the great awakening in England during the 1700s, the Welsh revival of 1904, or the Hebridian revival of the 40s & 50s, or even modern renewal / revival movements of the recent years in the USA and UK, the key issue has always been one grasped by some, and missed by others. It is the issue of a deep knowing of Jesus and our joining to Him, and He to us. Yet in the midst of outpouring the words, *'Eat my flesh...'* are still as costly and offensive today as they were when originally spoken. Our soulish appetites still long for the peripheral activities of God, rather than the heart of Him who provides. Yes, it *is* God who moves in supernatural ways, and we rejoice in His great power, but if we do not become a 'Jesus person', or become a 'Jesus people', we can still die in our vain wandering in a kind of spiritual wilderness when in fact we were called like Israel to *'go in and possess...'*

The Lord in Deuteronomy 8: 3, spoke regarding His miraculous power given for His people, and yet gave them the 'deeper meaning' of the bread given for them.

"And feeding you with manna... to teach you that man does not live on bread alone but on every word that comes from the mouth of Lord..."

The mouth that spoke this to the children of Israel is the same mouth of the one God-man who spoke after the feeding of the five & four thousand, and the meaning is the same.

A deeper meaning still.

In the same chapter of John, the allusion is made to the forefathers of Israel who ate of this provision from heaven, and died in the wilderness. This people were uniquely called of God to an apostolic type ministry, led by Moses. They were called out of Egypt, to prove God's delivering power. They were called through the wilderness, to know of the leading of the Angel of the Lord. They were called to be a priestly people of a unique Kingdom, carrying the Ark of the Presence. But the ultimate purpose of all of this was to go into the land of promise, dispossess the nations, and establish God's true reign. What an awesome calling and destiny, and yet they failed because they could not fully identify with the Lord God, His righteous ways, His purpose, and the unique role they had in pointing ahead to the Messiah of God - Jesus! Paul in 1 Corinthians 10, warns the Church of the same tendency at work in them. He says:

"They all ate the same spiritual food... Nevertheless God was not pleased with most of them." **(V3 - 5)**

By the way, neither did Moses and Aaron go in! Despite their apostolic-type calling, they disobeyed the Lord.

The sober warning is this. God is now about to bring a fresh move of His glory, power and presence into the Church again. Jesus is the One providing a new outpouring of grace. The people of God today are knowing of heavenly manna. However, Jesus, will not fail to enter that promise with His people, in the way Moses did. His intention is that those that are 'in Him' will go in too. Therefore, whatever He is now pouring out is for that one aim alone, to create a 'Jesus people' who will no longer wander aimlessly in the wilderness and die, but rather go in! Jesus people are those that eat of Him, and DO NOT DIE! They, in their union and identification with Him, go where He goes. His destiny is theirs. This is the deeper and ultimate meaning of revival in every generation, and definitely today's! Young person don't miss it at this point, it is central to the Spirit's work. People may make of revival-type things what they will but the Spirit of God has this central issue in His heart - to create a Jesus generation. 'Jesus people' go in! They are of a resurrection kind and they do not wander or die. Don't miss the meaning of His outpouring - it has deep purpose in it!

Eating Him means identification not isolation.
This issue is not just a matter for the individual in becoming a 'Jesus person' but it is a corporate one. It is about a people embracing Christ and His Kingdom as a unique body of called-out ones on the earth. This is not so much an ecumenical 'all are involved' kind of calling where anything goes; in fact it is a particularly unique and exclusive one. Yes all are welcome but because of Christ's demands for our soul, our life, our all, it is a very **particular** thing to become a 'Jesus people'. Yes, Jesus prayed for unity among His congregation, but *centred solely around a fellowship **with** and **in** His dynamic*

person. We have been guilty of watering down the uniqueness of the man Jesus. We have preached mental assent to Christ in order to get people 'saved' rather than the original concept of becoming His and joining Him in His exodus. God forgive us!

One of the key moments in a disciple's life is the moment of his calling to follow. That's how it was in the life of Andrew & Peter, Phillip & Nathanael. It was deemed so important that John in his Gospel (Chapter 1: 35 - 51) gives a lengthy account of their time of forsaking all to follow Christ. Andrew, after hearing John the Baptist's words, 'Look the Lamb of God', goes to find his brother Simon Peter, and ceases from being John the Baptist's disciple and becomes a dedicated pursuer of Jesus. The same is true of

Phillip who goes to find Nathanael. They both leave all to follow. What is the meaning of this? It is simple. For them, believing in Jesus meant identity with Him, and it was all or nothing for them. They became a 'Jesus people'. They became the 'ekklesia' (called-out ones) of God, in Jesus. For them this was eating the bread of Him who came to bring eternal life. Yet today, things are often different. 'Becoming a Christian' is about a mental assent to the right thing or doctrine. "Jesus Christ is my saviour, He died for my sins; I am forgiven and am going to heaven." And then the individual remains the same, isolated, and never enters 'into God'. They fail to eat His flesh and drink His blood until He is in very union with them. Their identity *in and with the Master* is not grasped.

Some have said because of the influence of this western-type individualistic centred message, *"Faith in Jesus is a personal thing. I don't need to come to meet with God's people. I can have my faith where I am."* I was confronted with these words when visiting Poland, after one young lady had had dramatic experience of Jesus, only after which the enemy came and robbed her with the following deception. She believed that because her new 'faith' was a personal issue of forgiveness and granting access to heaven alone, that she did not need to become a key member with God's people. She could not grasp the costly demands of identity with Jesus the Master, and all that faith in Him meant. I was deeply troubled by these words and did not know how to answer them. I did not want to come up with the spiritual clichés of how we need to meet together as the Church etc. I wanted God's answer, not only for that situation but for wherever we proclaim the Gospel. After days of seeking, the truth suddenly came alive in me. I began to see that to the early disciples believing in the Gospel was not just a matter of personal forgiveness (though we have that). I became aware that our Gospel preaching in the West had become focused on the individual benefits from God to us, and it had produced an 'individualistic salvation'. I became aware that the first century concept of the Gospel was in stark contrast to the one today. We preach justification without identification, and we teach baptism as symbolic of 'new life' without emphasising the individual's immersion into Jesus and His body. The results of this are disastrous, and are sadly evident in churches across the UK, USA & other neo-western countries today.

We have missed the essence of our salvation, which is in the account of the feeding of the thousands - i.e. the Bread of Life must be eaten and recognised for who He is, so that we become part of that one body / loaf. To see God's miraculous power alone is great, but insufficient if we fail to become a true 'Jesus person' and join with a true 'Jesus people', of whom all are inseparably linked to this glorious God-man. This is what that young lady in Poland had failed to see. Again, with the words of Jesus I ask: *"Do you still not understand?"*

The Bread of Presence.
The amazing thing about the command to 'eat

the flesh' of Jesus is that it contains not only an experience of identity with Him, but also a knowing of Him with us, *"...and I in him"* - **(John 6: 56)**

So there is a remaining in Him on our part, but also of Him in us on His part. When we eat bread in the natural we eat and enjoy its taste. It goes down into our digestive system, giving of its nutrients, and if you like, it becomes a part of us. This is the case with those that eat the flesh of the Son of Man. It is a guarantee of His presence - always. The bread to be kept in the tabernacle in Exodus was called, 'the Bread of Presence', and the bread we eat in communion is a celebration of the same reality - our union with Him, and He with us. It is to be experienced, tasted and known. Whilst many have said that feelings are not what following Christ is about, I find the deeper I look into what Jesus' life and message was about, the more I see that it was all about a true & living experience that is entered into through faith. This is what He called men into. Praise King Jesus!

Finally… Mark's insight on the issue.

And so now we return to Mark's account in chapter 8 of the second miracle of this two-part act from Jesus. As in the first miracle, there are similar themes:

- Belief and unbelief.
- Obedience and disobedience.
- Signs in and of themselves versus signs that penetrate the heart and lead to Christ.
- Wander and die during visitation or go into King-centred identity during visitation.

Mark puts the emphasis on Jesus' questions to His followers. *'Are you hard of hearing? Are you blind? Do you still not understand?'*

What are they not getting? Firstly, there is significance in bread. There is bread which contains yeast, causing it to rise. In the Exodus, God commanded Israel to make bread without yeast in order to have a quick escape from Egypt. They would not have time to wait for the yeast to grow. So to Israel yeast was a sign of holding onto former ways, worldliness, disobedience and sin. Jesus is saying here that those who are identified with Him and are one in Him, are like a loaf without yeast, for He is not of Egypt but of the land of promise. The people that went in to the land were those who believed, obeyed, captured the heart of God's activities and were those who took into the new land His Kingly rule and presence. They are those who will not hold on to former things but embrace His ways. Therefore the manifestation of Herod and the Pharisees sinfulness is like yeast in the people of Israel that did not enter the promise. A little leaven leavens the whole lump. God's Old Testament congregation Israel was now leavened, yet Christ had come to form a new people of God - His called out ones, in whom no yeast dwells – *they are to know Him*! In other words, the deeper meaning of the visitation and outpouring of the Spirit is the light of Christ's righteousness that shines through those who embrace the heart and depth of what's happening. Unrighteousness and unbelief cannot enter into the promise of God. Jesus people do, because their Master has already stepped into the promise!

So today's application is simple: The unrighteous do not believe or go after identity with Jesus, but they want to keep the supernatural provision. The righteous believe, they gladly lay down all for this union with Jesus, and they experience His Kingdom reign and know fruitfulness. They in their allegiance *will* go in. *Do we now understand?*

Finally, Christ also puts an emphasis on the number of baskets left over and the connection between the two events. Here is a glorious ministry of Jesus to the Jew and Gentile. Scholars agree that the first was to a Jewish audience, the second feeding to both Jew and Gentile.[1] Now in God's new day of visitation, through His Son, Gentiles become part of the congregation of God, with Jews, to go **into the promise land and carry** the Kingdom. The One new man is a reality through Him. This is what the Spirit is now calling for in this fresh move of His Spirit. Hence in Mark 8 the mention of only one loaf in the boat after the miracle. Out of the Jew & Gentile He forms a 'Jesus people.'

So this is the meaning of the Bread of Heaven.
- It is to be eaten - that is absorbed into our spirits, through identification with Jesus, and by the Holy Spirit's entrance into our hearts. Remember, you are what you eat. No yeast in this bread.
- It's meaning is also exclusively Jesus-centred not 'sign-centred'. Yet out of this union, great Kingdom demonstration is evidenced.

- It's meaning is about a body of people, who embrace the above, who in fellowship and apostolic movement form God's new people. Thus they are called to inherit and dispossess nations. We are to be led by the Angel of the Lord who is the Lord Jesus. We are now to carry the Ark of His presence in our hearts. We are to experience supernatural signs of power but also grasp their significance. They are signs of the Kingdom! HOWEVER, we are not to die, for those in Christ do not die but live, they know, they do, they *are* - I.e. they 'go into promise'. This is a King-centred move of the Spirit - let's not forget it.

David Ravenhill has in recent years written timely words for these days of visitation we live in:

'How could Israel ever forget this incredible sight as they stood there on the banks of the Red Sea? They watched the entire Egyptian army being swallowed up by the mighty torrents of water cascading down upon them. God was unleashing His mighty hand of judgment against those who had helped impose Israel's forced captivity of oppression and slavery... As wonderful as this experience was, it was merely the beginning – the first step in God's plan and purpose for His people. Even as they celebrated, God had His goal in mind – to "bring them and plant them in the mountain of (His) inheritance." (Exodus 15: 17) His purpose was to have people passionately in love with Him, a people who shared His heart for others who were in slavery and bondage.

This then, was the first stage in God's plan to

bring Israel out of their bondage; through the wilderness of testing, growth and preparation; and into the land of promise, where they would dwell in the very presence of God... God's plan was to bring His people into Zion and establish them in a life that revolved around His presence... The same thing is true for the Church... His ultimate goal is to gather all nations to Himself.' [2]

So one more time, with the words of Jesus, I repeat, *"Do you still not understand?"* He's moving again out of His great compassion, grace and favour. He is visiting His people but His deep callings remain the same, and if anything, during times of revival the intensity and power of those deep callings increase.

Jesus has come as 'Emmanuel - God with us' to reveal a deep and great mystery for all ages, that despite satan's assault on mankind, God can and will have a people for Himself. They as one new man will demonstrate what the early disciples became through their association with Jesus. The Jewish disciples of a Jewish Jesus accomplished what their ancestors did not, not because of their own ability but because of their identity in and with this glorious God-man, who is greater than Moses and succeeds where even Moses failed. *Let's not make the mistake of disassociating the power of God from the God of power. He moves in signs and wonders in order to reveal His heart, and for us to share in His heart.*

Today the prophetic call is the same and to this end. Today the apostolic mandate and mission is the same and to this end.

In the challenging words of Bob Gladstone, '*A new Jesus people are arising…*'

Will you become part of the new 'Jesus people'?

Appendix 1. What now?

If whilst reading this book, you have felt the stirrings of the Lord, or maybe God has spoken to you, my advice to you is this - *'whatever He says to you do it.'* However, that doesn't license you to become a spiritual maverick. Too many young people are floating around from church to church at this time in the West. The roots of today's young Christians are not deep enough and as a result there is no lasting fruit. I believe, despite the ineffective state of Western Christianity right now, that God is still working in His people, through His Church and God still has His servants at work in leadership in various local churches as a whole. Pray to God for humility and meekness. Study the Word. Speak with your leaders about how you can become the disciple God wants you to be. Don't criticise the impurity and darkness in the Church but become the salt and light that it needs. Don't become frustrated because of the lack of fire in the Church, but spark a flame! I appreciate that there may be some of you reading this book and you are maybe involved in a church that doesn't even preach the Gospel, or maybe there is no heart for a move of God's Spirit, worse still, maybe has no spiritual leadership. My counsel to you is, again - don't become a spiritual rebel (there's no such thing anyway!), but if your church does not preach or believe the truth and power of the Gospel then find a local Church that does, and come under its leaders and serve. Acknowledge that no local church is perfect, and that despite the imperfections, give yourself to making a difference in that place in a humble and submitted way. If you are a part of Gospel church, then speak with your leaders about how you long for God to work in you and serve with the people there. If you attend a Church where there is no Biblical leadership then my advice is to belong to somewhere that does and give yourself.

Maybe there are those of you whom God is calling to a season of preparation for service. Ask your leaders about how you can train or be mentored. But do whatever it takes to make a difference in your generation. Make sure all your fleshly ambitions, desires and attitudes are nailed to the Cross - then in the power of the Holy Spirit become a blazing vessel in the Master's hands. Do not settle for the mediocre!

Appendix 2. Recommended Reading.

Just before finalising this book's content, I had an idea that was a little different to the norm, and yet one I considered needful. It occurred to me that I needed to include a list of recommended books for further reading, for all the young people reading this book, who have a genuine longing for the Lord. (More fuel for the fire so to speak.) Generally I have tried to list the books that have impacted my life regarding some of the themes mentioned in this book. Please also be aware that the books listed are only those that I believe to be still obtainable. There are many other, older and greater titles that I would have loved to include but many of these are incredibly difficult to locate. So below, here is the unconventional second Appendix to the book. But I finish with the words of Leonard

Ravenhill adapted by myself:

"Don't just go through these books but let these books go through you!"

- *George Whitefield's Journals.*
- *Hudson Taylor's Spiritual Secret - Dr. and Mrs H Taylor.*
- *Why Revival Tarries - Leonard Ravenhill*
- *'Revolution' & 'Revolution in the Church' - Michael L. Brown*
- *Your Sons and Daughters shall prophesy - Ernest Gentile*
- *Radical Christian - Arthur Wallis.*
- *Pathway to Pentecost - Samuel Chadwick.*
- *The Gospel of the Kingdom - George Eldon Ladd.*
- *Apostolic Foundations – Art Katz.*
- *THE BIBLE!*

Notes.

Chapter 1.

[i] The Journey (A Lifetime of Prophetic Moments), written by Dick Iverson (City Christian Publishing, October 1995) Use of sub - title of book.

Chapter 2.

[1] Quote taken from Hugh Blacks final message entitled 'We would see Jesus' spoken at Struthers Memorial Church, Scotland.

[2] Henry, Matthew, *Matthew Henry's Commentary on the Bible* (Marshall, Morgan & Scott 1960) Quote from commentary on 2nd Corinthians 5: 1 - 11 - P629

[3] Ibid. P424 - 425. Not directly quoted but was blessed as God spoke to my heart about this story, that Henry had compiled thoughts of a similar kind.

[4] C.T. Studd - Cricketer and Pioneer, Norman Grubb (Lutterworth Press 1933) Quote taken from Chapter 6: P48.

Chapter 3.

[1] The Gospel of the Kingdom, George Eldon Ladd (Eerdmans 1959) Quotes taken from Chapter 9: P124 & 125. Ladd in my opinion has had Divine revelation on the subject of the Kingdom.

[2] Gospel and Spirit - Issues in NT Hermeneutics, Gordon Fee (Hendrikson 1991) P105 - 119. Fee argues that despite the various technical disputes in the Church, that the Pentecostals are absolutely right regarding the need of the present day seeking and experiencing the Spirit's Baptism.

[3] Apostolic Foundations, Arthur Katz (Burning Bush Press 1999) Quote taken from Chapter 2: P63 - 64

Chapter 4.

[1] LaSor quotation found in David Guzik's Online Bible Commentary (www.enduringword.com accessed 2005 and January 2007)

[2] Word definition taking from 1st Edition of American Dictionary of the English Language, Noah Webster.

[3] William Lane, NICNT on the Gospel of Mark (Eerdmans Publishing Company, 1974) Lane is quoting from K. Rengstorf, TWNT, P400 - 430

Chapter 5.

[1] Apostolic Foundations, Arthur Katz (Burning Bush Press 1999) Quote taken from Chapter 2: P65

[2] Ibid P65 - 66

[3] Quote taken from message entitled 'The Spirit and the Cross' as part of an audio series entitled: 'The Kingdom, Spirit and the People of God.' spoken by Gordon Fee at Regents College 1999.

Chapter 6.

[1] Quote taken from song 'Jesus Lover of my soul (It's all about You, Jesus)' written by Paul Oakley. 1995 EMI Christian Music / Kingsway's Thankyou Music.

[ii] Leaning into the wind, A.W. Tozer (Send the Light Books 1985) Quote taken from Chapter 1: P18

Chapter 7.

[1] William Lane, NICNT on the Gospel of Mark (Eerdmans Publishing Company, 1974) Comments on Mark 8 account of feeding of 4000.

[2] They drank from the river and died in the wilderness, David Ravenhill (Destiny Image 2000) Quote taken from Chapter 6: P67 & 68

Printed in the United Kingdom
by Lightning Source UK Ltd.
134227UK00001B/124-165/P